PHOTOGRAPHY YEARBOOK 1992

INTERNATIONALES JAHRBUCH DER FOTOGRAFIE 1992

PHOTOGRAPHY YEARBOOK

1992

INTERNATIONALES JAHRBUCH DER FOTOGRAFIE 1992

edited by
Peter Wilkinson *FRPS*

Fountain Press

Fountain Press Limited
Queensborough House
2 Claremont Road
Surbiton
Surrey KT6 4QU
England

Designed by Sally Stockwell

Reproduction and Printing by
Regent Publishing Services Ltd
Hong Kong

Deutsche Ausgabe:
© 1991 Wilhelm Knapp Verlag,
Niederlassung der Droste Verlag GmbH, Düsseldorf.
ISBN 3-87420-172-4

contents

INTRODUCTION

As the Editor of PHOTOGRAPHY YEARBOOK I have to make what I sometimes find to be difficult decisions on what type of photograph should or should not be included in the book. For this edition, we received, for the first time as far as I can recollect, a number of hand-coloured prints — or, to be more precise, black-and-white prints which had been hand-coloured in local areas. These in some cases produced most intriguing images. So did some of the photo-montages submitted — pictures produced from more than one original either by pasting parts of prints together and re-photographing the end result, or by combining colour transparencies. In the end I decided to include one or two not very obvious montages but to exclude any hand-coloured pictures.

Another new approach in image-making, as far as the YEARBOOK is concerned, is for the artist/photographer to compose a picture out of a number of objects and then photograph the result, either in a straightforward way or with distorted perspective. Obviously the result is a photograph, but there is a widely held view that, if it is a straight copy, it is like a painter photographing one of his paintings and submitting it as a photograph. Provided, however, that the pictures have photographic merit, I enjoy viewing some of these artificial but highly creative and visually exciting images, and The Royal Photographic Society of Great Britain ensured that such work would be seen by a wider audience by having a number of exhibitions of this type of work during 1991.

This brings me to the question of where creative photography is going and what will be accepted as a 'photograph' in the future. A most exciting 1991 calendar was that of Canon Europa N.V., which is made up of twelve sport-orientated impressions. These were originally photographs, but American artist Jim Valentine, using a Color Laser Copier and a Bubble Jet Copier, transformed them into highly imaginative and individual compositions. I suspect that not much hand-work was involved, but Canon refer to the end results as paintings, not photographs. Bearing in mind the origin of the images, though, I am not sure that this is the correct description.

I believe that in the future we will see much closer links between the art and craft of conventional photography and the controlled electronic imagery produced by colour copiers, etc., and that the definition of photography which I have always accepted — that it is basically the action of light and chemicals on sensitive material to create an objective or subjective image — will become outdated. But for this edition of PHOTOGRAPHY YEARBOOK, the pictures selected conform to the traditional definition.

Once again, for this edition, hundreds of photographers from nearly forty countries supported the YEARBOOK by submitting thousands of prints and colour transparencies — in fact, the Publisher believes that it was the greatest number of entries ever. And again we were pleased to receive many from Eastern Europe. In my capacity as Editor I congratulate all successful contributors, for with so many submissions it is an even greater achievement to have had work accepted this year.

The Publisher, who as usual has taken a lot of trouble to ensure that the quality of reproduction of the photographs is as high as possible, and I thank everyone who sent work for possible inclusion, and request you to submit your best photographs for the next edition. It is only with the continuing support of amateur and professional photographers worldwide that PHOTOGRAPHY YEARBOOK has existed since 1935.

The closing date for receiving material at the publishers for possible inclusion in the next edition of PHOTOGRAPHY YEARBOOK is the end of January 1992. Colour transparencies may be of any size but should not be glass-mounted. If a colour picture is available both as a print and as a transparency, we would prefer the transparency. Prints, both black-and-white and colour, should be unmounted and not smaller than 18×24cm or larger than 30×40cm. Prints should always be packed flat, not rolled. All work submitted must carry the author's name and any information as to the location and other facts of interest relating to the picture, as well as to the make of camera, lens and film used.

If packing is suitable, and sufficient return postage in sterling cheques or money orders is included, work will be returned after the book has been finalised. All possible care will be taken by Fountain Press, but they cannot be held responsible for any loss or damage that might occur to material submitted. Although the copyright of any work accepted remains with the author, the publisher may use accepted pictures to publicise PHOTOGRAPHY YEARBOOK.

As well as enjoying the prestige of having their work published, successful contributors will receive a copy of PHOTOGRAPHY YEARBOOK and a reproduction fee. Upon request the publishers will, where possible, put prospective picture buyers in touch with the authors of successful pictures.

We hope that you enjoy the 1992 PHOTOGRAPHY YEARBOOK and will submit, and encourage others to submit, suitable material for possible inclusion in the next edition. Pictures from photographers outside the United Kingdom are especially welcome as they help to maintain the book's international character.

Peter Wilkinson, FRPS

EINFÜHRUNG

Als Herausgeber des Internationalen Jahrbuchs der Fotographie muß ich mitunter schwierige Entscheidungen treffen, welche Art Bilder in diesem Buch erscheinen sollen und welche nicht. Wir erhielten für diese Ausgabe, soweit ich mich erinnern kann, erstmalig eine Anzahl handkolorierter Aufnahmen oder genauer gesagt Schwarz/Weiß Fotos, die in gewißen Stellen von Hand koloriert worden waren. Diese Aufnahmen zeigten in einigen Fällen sehr aufregende Gestaltung, ebenso wie einige der eingereichten Fotomontagen — Fotos, die aus mehr als einem Original entstehen, teilweise zusammengemischt werden, um als Endresultat neu fotografiert zu werden oder durch Kombination von Farbdias. Letztendlich entschied ich, ein oder zwei nicht allzu offensichtliche Montagen zu inkludieren aber jegliche handkolorierte Fotos auszuschliessen.

Ein weiterer neuer Schritt für die Schaffung von Bildern ist, was dieses Jahrbuch betrifft, jener Vorgang, bei welchem der Künstler/Fotograf ein Bild aus mehreren Objekten schafft und das Resultat entweder in gewohnter direkter Weise oder mit verzogenen Perspektiven fotografiert. Offensichtlich ist dieses Resultat ein Foto, aber es besteht die weitverbreitete Meinung, daß, sofern es sich um eine direkte Aufnahme handelt, dieses einem Foto gleichgesetzt werden muß, das ein Maler von seinem Gemälde macht und dann als Fotografie präsentiert. Vorausgesetzt, daß diese Bilder fotografischen Wert besitzen, erfreue ich mich am Betrachten einiger dieser konstruierten, aber höchst kreativen und visuell aufregenden Bilder und "The Royal Photographic Society of Great Britain" (Die königliche Gesellschaft der Fotografie in Großbritannien) hat versichert, daß solcherlei Arbeiten einem weiteren Publikum zugänglichgemacht werden sollen, indem im Jahre 1991 einige Ausstellungen mit Arbeiten dieser Art abgehalten werden.

Das bringt mich zu der Frage wohin sich kreative Fotografie entwickelt und was in Zukunft als "Fotografie" akzeptiert werden kann. Äußerst interessant war der 1991 Kalender von Canon Europa N.V., der zwölf Aufnahmen aus dem Sportleben darstellt. Diese waren ursprünglich Fotografien, aber der amerikanische Künstler Jim Valentine verwandelte sie unter Verwendung eines Laserfarbkopierers und eines Blasenstrahldruckers zu höchst kreativen und individuellen Kompositionen. Ich glaube, daß nicht sehr viel Handarbeit involviert war, aber Canon bezeichnet die Endresultate als Gemälde und ich als Fotografien. Vom Original der Bilder ausgehend bin ich nicht sicher, ob dies die richtige Beschreibung ist.

Ich prophezeihe für die Zukunft eine viel engere Bindung zwischen Kunst und Handwerk der konventionellen Fotografie und den elektronisch kontrollierten Bildern, die durch Farbkopierer etc. hergestellt werden, und daß die Definition von Fotografie, die für mich immer die Aktion von Licht und chemischen Elementen auf empfindlichem Material zur Kreierung eines objektiven oder subjektiven Eindrucks war, überholt ist. Aber für diese Ausgabe des Internationalen Jahrbuchs der Fotografie jedoch entsprechen alle ausgewählten Aufnahmen der traditionellen Definition.

Wieder einmal haben Fotografen aus nahezu vierzig Ländern das Jahrbuch unterstützt und Tausende von Abzügen und Farbdias eingereicht. Der Herausgeber glaubt sogar, daß noch nie soviele Arbeiten eingereicht wurden. Und wieder waren wir sehr erfreut, eine große Teilnahme aus den Osteuropäischen Ländern verzeichnen zu können. Ich möchte in meiner Funktion als Herausgeber allen erfolgreichen Einsendern herzlich gratulieren, da es bei einer so großen Teilnahme dieses Jahr noch ehrenvoller ist, wenn eine Arbeit akzeptiert wurde.

Der Verleger, der wie immer größte Sorgfalt in der Reproduktion der Fotografien walten ließ, um bestmögliche Qualität zu garantieren und ich danken all jenen, die ihre Arbeiten für mögliche Veröffentlichung eingesandt haben und bitten Sie, auch für die nächste Ausgabe Ihre besten Werke einzusenden. Nur aufgrund der anhaltenden Unterstützung von Amateur und Berufsfotografen aus aller Welt konnte das Internationalen Jahrbuch der Fotografie seit 1935 bestehen.

Einsendeschluß für Material, das möglicherweise in der nächsten Ausgabe des Internationalen Jahrbuchs der Fotografie veröffentlicht wird, ist Ende Januar 1992. Zu diesem Zeitpunkt muß das Material beim Verleger eingelangt sein. Farbtransparente können von jeglicher Größe sein, dürfen jedoch nicht in Glasrahmen gesandt werden. Sollte ein Farbbild als Abzug und als Farbtransparent vorhanden sein, bitten wir um Einsendung des Dias. Alle Fotos — sowohl Schwarz/Weiß als auch Farb — sollen nicht aufgezogen, nicht kleiner als 18 × 24cm und nicht größer als 30 × 40cm sein. Abzüge sollen immer flach verpackt und nicht gerollt werden. Alle eingesandten Arbeiten müssen den Namen des Fotografen tragen, sowie Informationen über Aufnahmeort, spezielle Interessensfaktoren in Bezug auf die Aufnahme und vor allem Angaben über die verwendete Kamera, Linse und Film enthalten.

Wenn das Verspackungsmaterial entspricht und ausreichendes Retourporto in Form von Schecks in Englischen Pfunden oder Internationalen Antwortscheinen beigelegt ist, werden Arbeiten nach Verlagsabschluß des Buches retourniert. Fountain Press wird selbstverständlich alle arbeiten mit größter Sorgfalt behandeln, kann jedoch keinerlei Haftung für eventuelle Beschädigung oder Verluste des eingesandten Materials übernehmen. Wenn auch das Urheberrect der eingesandten Arbeiten dem Einsender zusteht, darf der Verleger angenommene Arbeiten im Internationalen Jahrbuch der Fotografie veröffentlichen.

Abgesehen vom Prestige ihre Arbeiten veröffentlicht zu sehen, werden erfolgreiche Teilnehmer auch eine Ausgabe des Internationalen Jahrbuchs der Fotografie und eine Reproduktionsgebühr erhalten. Auf Anfrage wird sich der Verlag bemühen, zukünftige Fotokäufer und Schöpfer erfolgreicher Bilder zusammenzuführen.

Wir hoffen, daß Sie am Internationalen Jahrbuch der Fotografie 1992 Freude haben und auch in Zukunft Ihre Arbeiten für mögliche Publikation in der nächsten Ausgabe einsenden werden. Fotos von Fotografen außerhalb Großbritanniens sind uns besonders willkommen, da diese helfen, den Internationalen Charakter dieses Buches aufrechtzuerhalten.

Peter Wilkinson, FRPS

INTRODUCTION

En ma qualité d'éditeur du PHOTOGRAPHY YEARBOOK je me trouve parfois obligé de prendre des décisions difficiles quant au genre de photographies à inclure dans ce livre. En vue de la présente édition, nous avons reçu, pour la première fois, autant que je me souvienne, un certain nombre d'épreuves coloriées à la main — ou, pour être plus précis, des épreuves en blanc et noir dont certaines parties avaient été coloriées à la main. De telles épreuves avaient produit dans certains cas de très curieuses images. Il en était de même de certains photo-montages qui nous ont été soumis: il s'agissait d'images composées au moyen de plusieurs épreuves originales, soit en collant des morceaux d'épreuves et en rephotographiant le résultat, soit en combinant des diapositives en couleurs. J'ai finalement décidé d'inclure un ou deux montages point trop évidents, mais d'exclure toutes les épreuves coloriées à la main.

Il y a aussi une autre nouvelle approche de la fabrication d'images en ce qui concerne le PHOTOGRAPHY YEARBOOK: l'artiste — le photographe — compose une image à l'aide d'un certain nombre d'objets, puis photographie l'ensemble, soit tel quel, soit en déformant la perspective. Il est bien évident que le résultat est une photographie, mais nombre de gens estiment que lorsqu'il s'agit d'une copie pure et simple, c'est comme si un peintre photographiait ses tableaux et présentait le résultat comme une photographie. A condition cependant qu'elles présentent certain mérite photographique, j'aime regarder certaines des images ainsi produites, artificielles certes, mais d'une réelle créativité, et visuellement très intéressantes; et la Royal Photographic Society of Great Britain a fait en sorte que de tels travaux puissent être vus par un public plus large en organisant au cours de l'année 1991 un certain nombre d'expositions d'oeuvres de cette nature.

Ceci m'amène à la question de savoir où va la photographie, et ce qui sera accepté à l'avenir comme photographie. Il existe un calendrier pour l'année 1991 de la Canon Europa N.V. composé de douze impressions de sport. Celles-ci étaient à l'origine des photographies, mais l'artiste américain Jim Valentine à l'aide d'un 'Color Laser Copier' et d'un 'Bubble Jet Copier' les a transformées en compositions d'une grande originalité et d'une haute qualité d'imagination. Je doute qu'il y ait eu là beaucoup de travail de sa main, mais Canon appelle le résultat 'peintures' et non 'photographies'. Cependant, étant donné l'origine de ces images, je ne suis pas sûr que c'en soit une description correcte.

Je crois qu'à l'avenir nous assisterons à une union de plus en plus étroite entre l'art et le métier de la photographie traditionnelle d'une part, et la production d'images électroniquement controlée par des duplicateurs en couleurs, etc, et que la définition de la photographie que j'ai toujours acceptée — c'est-à-dire, essentiellement, l'action de la lumière et de produits chimiques sur une surface sensible pour créer une image objective ou subjective — va se trouver dépassée. Mais pour cette édition du PHOTOGRAPHY YEARBOOK les images choisies sont conformes à la définition traditionnelle.

Cette année encore, pour cette édition, des centaines de photographes de près de quarante pays ont apporté leur soutien au YEARBOOK en nous envoyant des milliers d'épreuves et de diapositives; en fait, les directeurs de Fountain Press croient bien n'en avoir jamais reçu un si grand nombre. Et cette année encore, nous sommes heureux d'une si large contribution des pays d'Europe de l'Est. En ma capacité d'éditeur, je félicite ceux dont les travaux ont été choisis: leur succès, cette année, est d'autant plus remarquable qu'ils l'emportent sur tant d'autres.

Les directeurs de Fountain Press, qui ont, comme toujours, fait de leur mieux pour assurer aux photographies la meilleure qualité de reproduction possible, et moi-même, remercions tous ceux qui ont envoyé leurs travaux pour une éventuelle inclusion, et nous les prions de nous soumettre leurs meilleures photographies pour notre prochaine édition. C'est seulement grâce au fidèle soutien des photographes amateurs et professionnels du monde entier que le PHOTOGRAPHY YEARBOOK existe depuis 1935.

La date limite pour la réception par la direction de Fountain Press des travaux soumis pour une éventuelle reproduction dans la prochaine édition du PHOTOGRAPHY YEARBOOK est le 31 janvier 1992. Les diapositives en couleurs peuvent être de n'importe quelles dimensions, mais ne doivent pas être montées sur verre; les épreuves, en blanc et noir et en couleurs, ne doivent pas être montées, et ne doivent pas mesurer moins de 18×24cm, ni plus de 30×40cm. Les épreuves doivent toujours être emballées à plat, et non roulées. Tous les travaux proposés doivent porter le nom de leur auteur, et l'indication du lieu et d'autres faits relatifs à l'image, à l'appareil, à l'objectif et à la pellicule utilisés.

Si l'emballage est convenable, et l'envoi accompagné des frais de port en chèque ou mandat sterling, les travaux seront réexpédiés à leurs auteurs une fois achevée la préparation du livre. Bien que tous les envois soient traités avec le plus grand soin, Fountain Press ne peut accepter la responsabilité d'aucune perte ou dommage survenu au matériel reçu. Bien que le copyright de toute photographies soit conservé par l'auteur, les éditeurs se réservent le droit de l'utiliser à des fins de publicité pour le PHOTOGRAPHY YEARBOOK. Les contributeurs dont les travaux sont reproduits non seulement jouiront du prestige que leur confère la publication dans le PHOTOGRAPHY YEARBOOK, mais aussi recevront un exemplaire du livre et un droit de reproduction. Sur requête, la direction de Fountain Press pourra se charger, là où la chose sera possible, de mettre en relation les éventuels acheteurs avec les auteurs des photographies publiées.

Nous espérons que vous prendrez plaisir au PHOTOGRAPHY YEARBOOK de 1992, et que vous nous soumettrez, et encouragerez vos amis à nous soumettre, des travaux susceptibles d'être reproduits dans notre prochaine édition. Les photographies proposées par des auteurs étrangers au Royaume-Uni sont particulièrement bienvenues parce qu'elles contribuent à conserver à cet ouvrage son caractère international.

Peter Wilkinson, FRPS

INTRODUCCION

Como autor de la presente edición del PHOTOGRAPHY YEARBOOK, me corresponde tomar lo que a veces son decisiones muy difíciles sobre qué tipo de fotografía debe ser incluida en el libro. Para esta edición recibimos, creo que por primera vez, unas cuantas copias coloreadas a mano. Mejor dicho, copias en blanco y negro con ciertas zonas coloreadas a mano. En algunos casos, estas copias producen imágenes sorprendentes, al igual que algunos de los fotomontajes que hemos recibido — fotografías producidas o bien montando varios originales juntos y fotografiándolos de nuevo, o bien combinando diversas transparencias en color. Finalmente decidí incluir uno o dos montajes no muy obvios y excluir las fotografías coloreadas a mano.

Otro nuevo enfoque en la producción de miágenes, en lo que se refiere al PHOTOGRAPHY YEARBOOK, es cuando el artista/fotógrafo compone una imagen combinando una serie de objetos que luego son fotografiados bien sea de forma normal o con perspectivas distorsionadas. Obviamente el resultado es una fotografía, pero la opinión general es que, si se trata de una simple copia, es como si un pintor fotografiase su obra y la presentase como fotografía. No obstante, si estas copias tienen mérito fotográfico, es un placer ver imágenes que, aunque artificiales, tienen un gran valor plástico y creativo. La Royal Photographic Society de Gran Bretaña ha hecho posible que dichas obras estén a la vista del público a lo largo de 1991, montando exposiciones específicamente dedicadas a este tipo de trabajo.

Esto me lleva a la pregunta de a dónde irá a parar la fotografía creativa y qué se entenderá en el futuro como "fotografía". Uno de los calendarios más interesantes de 1991 es el de Canon Europa N.V., el cual está compuesto de doce imágenes de orientación deportiva. Las ilustraciones originalmente eran fotografías, pero el artista norteamericano Jim Valentine las transformó en composiciones sumamente imaginatives e individuales mediante la utilización de Colour Laser Copier y Bubble Jet Copier. Sospecho que no requirieron mucho trabajo manual, pero Canon se refiere al resultado final como pinturas, no como fotografías. Teniendo en cuenta el orígen de las imágenes, no estoy seguro de que sea una descripción adecuada.

Pienso que en el futuro habrá una relación much más íntima entre la práctica convencional de la fotografía y aquellas imágenes controladas y producidas electrónicamente mediante copiadoras a color, etc. También pienso que la definición de fotografía que yo siempre he aceptado — la acción de la luz y de productos químicos sobre materiales sensibles para producir una imagen objetiva o subjetiva — quedará pronto pasada de moda. Pero para esta edición del PHOTOGRAPHY YEARBOOK las fotografías seleccionadas se ajustarán a la definición tradicional.

Una vez más, cientos de fotógrafos de casi cuarenta países prestaron su apoyo este año al PHOTOGRAPHY YEARBOOK y enviaron miles de fotografías y transparencias en color — de hecho, ha habido más participantes que nunca. Y una vez más, nos complace que un gran número de participantes proceda de Europa del este. Como autor de la edición, deseo felicitar a todos aquellos participantes que fueron seleccionados, ya que dado el gran número de obras presentadas es un logro aún mayor el haber sido sleccionado este año.

El editor, quien como siempre ha luchado para que las reproducciones fuesen de muy alta calidad, y yo queremos dar las gracias a todos los fotógrfos que nos enviaron sus obras para su posible inclusión, y rogarles que nos envíen sus mejores fotografías para la próxima edición. Es sólo gracias al apoyo continuo de los fotógrafos profesionales y aficionados del mundo entero que el PHOTOGRAPHY YEARBOOK sigue existiendo desde 1935.

El plazo para recibir material para su posible inclusión en la próxima edición del PHOTOGRAPHY YEARBOOK se cierra el 31 de enero de 1992. Las transparencias en color pueden ser de cualquier tamaño pero no montadas en vidrio. Si las fotografías en color existen como copia en papel y como transparencia, preferimos la transparencia. Las copias en papel, ya sean en blanco y negro o en color, deberán ir sin borde y tener un mínimo de 18×24cm. y un máximo de 30×40cm. Las copias en papel deberán ir siempre enviadas de forma plana, no enrolladas. Todas las obras presentadas llevarán el nombre del autor y cualquier tipo de información relativa al lugar o sujeto fotografiado, así como el tipo y marca de cámara, lente y película empleadas.

Si el embalaje es adecuado para su devolución y se cubren los gastos de envío, las obras serán devueltas una vez hecha la selección. Aunque se tomarán las medidas adecuadas, Fountain Press no se hace responsable de ninguna pérdida o daño que pueda sufrir el material. Aunque los derechos de autor sobre las obras seleccionadas seguirán en posesión del mismo, el editor se reserva el derecho a utilizarlas como publicidad del PHOTOGRAPHY YEARBOOK.

Los fotógrafos que sean seleccionados recibirán, además del prestigio de ser incluidos en sus páginas, una copia del PHOTOGRAPHY YEARBOOK y honorarios por cada reproducción. De ser requerido, y siempre que sea posible, la editorial pondrá en contacto a futuros compradores con los autores de las fotografías.

Esperamos que el PHOTOGRAPHY YEARBOOK sea de su agrado y nos envíe, y anime a otros a que nos envíen, material adecuado para su posible inclusión en la próxima edición. Las obras de fotógrafos procedentes de países fuera del Reino Unido son especialmente bienvenidas ya que ayudan a mantener el carácter internacional del libro.

Peter Wilkinson, FRPS

THE ROYAL PHOTOGRAPHIC SOCIETY

JOIN THE POWER BEHIND PHOTOGRAPHY

As a special offer, readers of 'PHOTOGRAPHY YEARBOOK' are being given the opportunity of three months free membership. Join the society now, and receive fifteen months membership for the price of twelve. Write now to the membership officer, THE ROYAL PHOTOGRAPHIC SOCEITY, Milsom Street, Bath BA1 1DN (Telephone 0225 462841 or Fax 0225 448688). Be sure to mark your request 'PYB 1992'.

Develop the potential of your photography — membership of The Royal Photographic Society is open to everyone, whether you are a total beginner, a dedicated amateur or a full time professional in the imaging world.

An action packed programme of over 250 events a year awaits you — workshops, lectures, masterclasses, conferences, field trips and you would be welcomed at every single event.

Achieve — many who joined as beginners are now Fellows of the Society. Take advantage of the support and encouragement readily available to work towards one of the Society's distinctions. Remember, if you are successful you can use the letters FRPS, ARPS or LRPS after your name.

Enjoy a choice of magazines — The Photographic Journal and the Journal of Photographic Science, both of which come free to every member.

Seize the opportunity to become part of a wide network of fellow photographers so you can meet and learn with some of Britain's most highly recognised practitioners.

Adventure into different areas of photography by joining the experts in 13 specialist groups — Archaeology and Heritage, Audio Visual, Colour, Contemporary, Film & Video, Historical, Holography, Imaging Science and Technology, Medical, Pictorial, Nature, Travel and Visual Journalism.

Explore the work of the earliest photographers in the Society's extensive and world famous collection of rare photographs, books, equipment and periodicals by Fox Talbot, Julia Margaret Cameron, Ansel Adams, Edward Weston, Yousef Karsch, Edward Steichen and many, many more.

Visit the Society's nationally recognised centre of photography in Bath, view at first hand exciting and stimulating work from historical and documentary images to the scientific and very avant garde. Immerse yourself in the comprehensive array of books, posters and postcards in the shop; make yourself at home in the members Club Room, or entertain in the restaurant. Bring a friend — entry is free to members and a guest.

And it doesn't matter where you live — there are 14 regions in Britain each with its own regional organiser and members in over 40 countries abroad, many of which have their own society representative.

THE PHOTOGRAPHERS

THE PHOTOGRAPHERS

INES ROBERTS

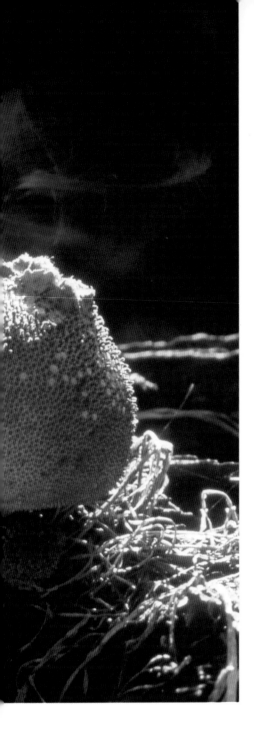

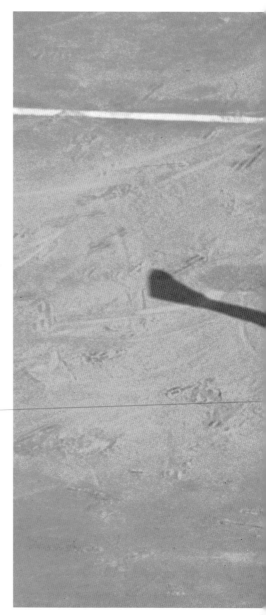

ARNOLD HUBBARD ▶

Daniel Motz

ARNOLD HUBBARD

BRETISLAV MAREK

DHIMAN BOSE

JANOS EIFERT

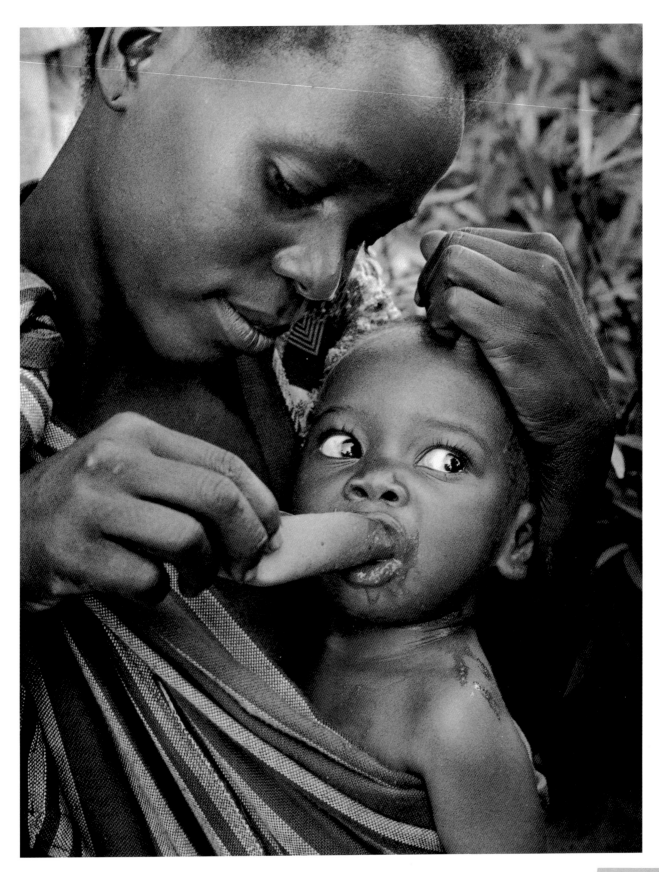

Jim Walker

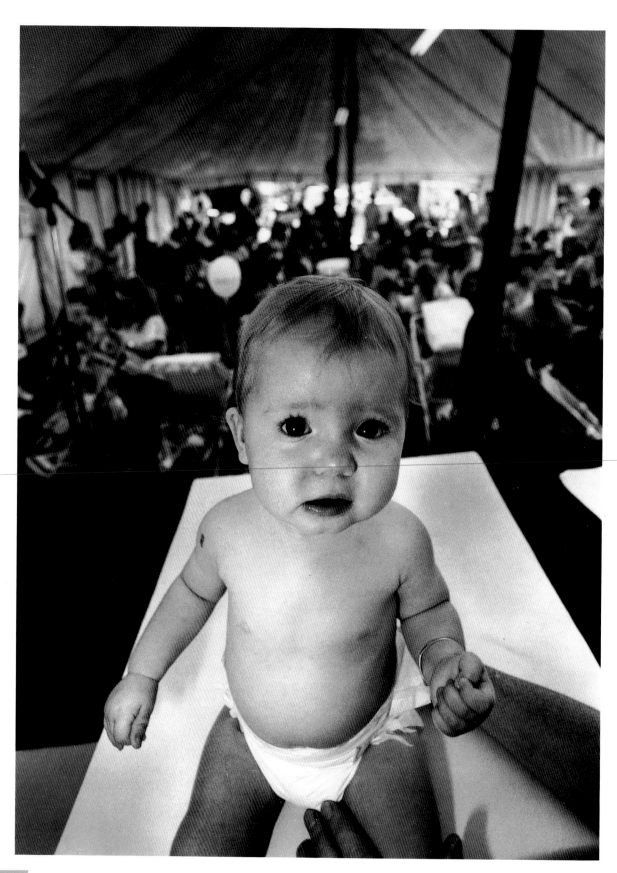

SZAMODY ZSOLT

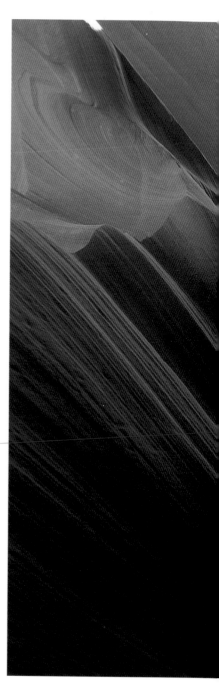

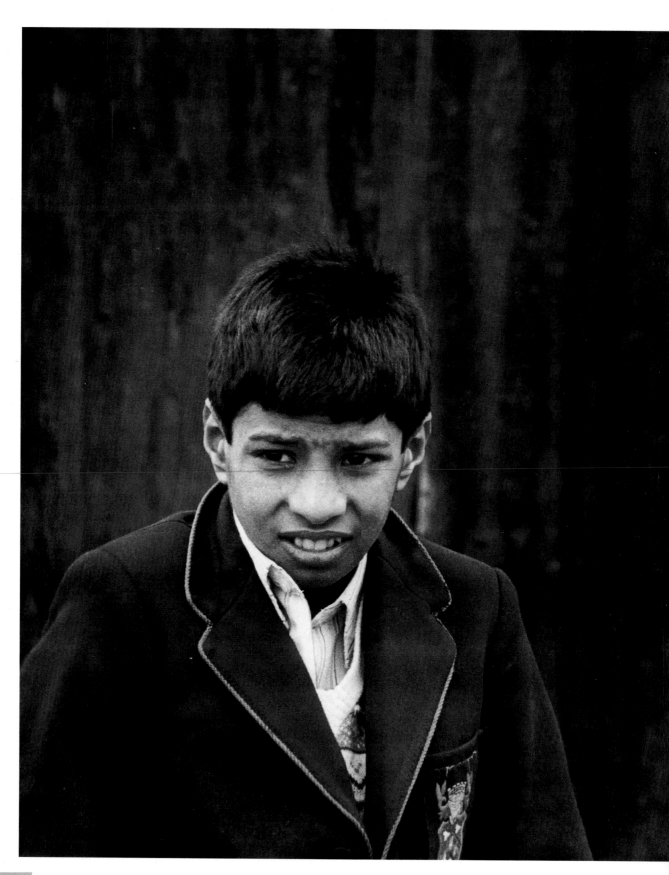

BILL IVY

PETER HALLAM

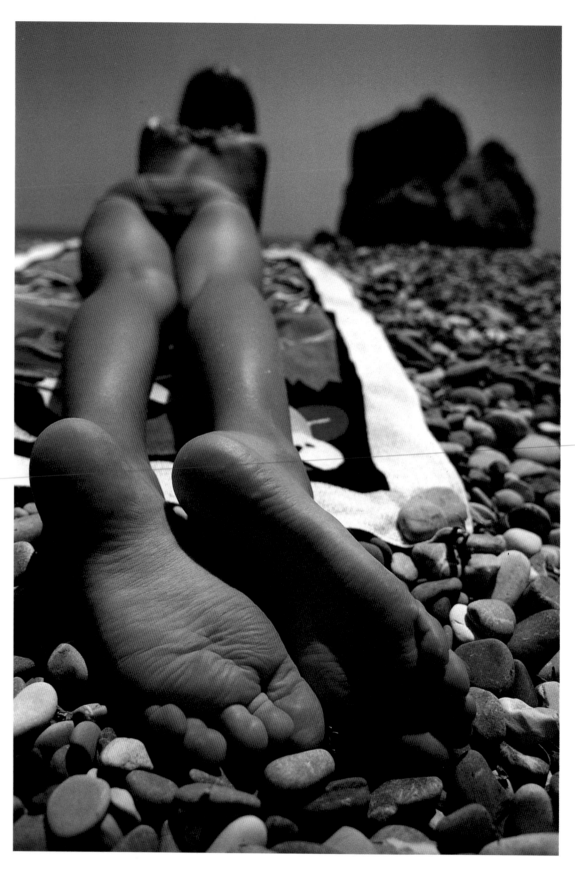

TONY BUTCHER

CLAUDIO MARCOZZI

P. GLYN-JONES

COVER

Photographer	Gwen Charnock (UK)
Subject/Location	Self Portrait taken behind glass previously sprayed with water
Camera	Nikon SA
Lens	Nikkor 105mm
Film	Ektachrome 100

FRONT END PAPER

Photographer	Leigh Preston (UK)
Subject/Location	Keithley, Yorkshire
Camera	Canon T90
Film	Ilford HPS

17

Photographer	Nigel Amies (UK)
Subject/Location	Asilah, Morocco
Camera	Nikon FE2
Lens	50mm
Film	Kodachrome 64

18

Photographer	P.E. Baldwin (UK)
Subject/Location	Guizhou, China

19

Photographer	P.E. Baldwin (UK)
Subject/Location	Gejia Girl, China

20

Photographer	Alan Brooke (UK)
Subject/Location	Jet Skier going over waterski jump – Thorpe Park
Camera	Nikon F801
Lens	24mm Nikkor with Metz Flashgun
Film	Fujichrome 100

21

Photographer	Alan Brooke (UK)
Subject/Location	Two girls having fun on a Yamaha watercraft on a lake near London
Camera	Nikon F301
Lens	Nikkor 18mm in underwater housing with remote triggering
Film	Fujichrome 100

22

Photographer	E.A. Janes (UK)
Subject/Location	Tawny Owl with house mouse – Hertfordshire, England
Camera	Hasselblad CM
Lens	250mm
Film	Fujichrome 50 with two flash heads

23

Photographer	E.A. Janes (UK)
Subject/Location	Wide mouth frog eating mouse, Hertfordshire, England
Camera	Hasselblad CM
Lens	150mm with extension tube
Film	Fujichrome 50

24-25

Photographer	Ines Roberts (USA)
Subject/Location	Photographer's daughter taken in Slot Canyon, Arizona, USA
Camera	Minolta XD5
Lens	70-210mm zoom
Film	Fujichrome 50

26

Photographer	J.J. Batten (UK)
Subject/Location	Empty warehouses, Regents Canal, Hackney, London
Camera	Olympos OM1
Lens	28mm Zuiko
Film	Kodachrome 25

27

Photographer	J.J. Batten (UK)
Subject/Location	Canalside buildings, Edmonton, London
Camera	Olympos OM1
Lens	28mm Zuiko
Film	Kodachrome 25

28

Photographer	Frank Young (UK)

29

Photographer	Derek Rodway (UK)

30

Photographer	Dan Smith (Allsport) (UK)
Subject/Location	Greg Norman – British Open Golf Tournament
Camera	Nikon

31

Photographer	Russell Cheyne (Allsport) (UK)
Subject/Location	Boris Becker at Monte Carlo Open
Camera	Nikon

32

Photographer	Peter Wilkinson (UK)
Subject/Location	Portrait taken afloat on East Coast, England
Camera	Canon A1
Lens	Sigma Zoom
Film	Fujicolor 200

33

Photographer	Arnold Hubbard (UK)
Subject/Location	Covent Garden, London
Camera	Nikon FE
Lens	55mm Nikkor
Film	Ilford XP1

34

Photographer	David Hall (UK)
Subject/Location	Co. Durham
Camera	Pentax K1000
Lens	80-200mm Zoom
Film	Kodak Plus-X

35

Photographer	Endrikas Juchka (USSR)

36

Photographer	H.S. Fonia (India)
Subject/Location	Himalaya, India
Camera	Canon AE1
Lens	55mm
Film	Orwo NP 22

37

Photographer	H.S. Fonia (UK)
Subject/Location	Joshi Matha, Himalaya, India
Camera	Canon AE1
Lens	55mm
Film	Orwo NP 22

38/39

Photographer	Daniel Motz (USA)
Subject/Location	Sarajevo, Yugoslavia
Camera	Nikon F3
Lens	135mm
Film	Kodak T. Max 400

40-41

Photographer	Victor Attfield (UK)
Subject/Location	Antique Shop, Yorkshire
Camera	Nikkormat FTN
Lens	28mm Nikkor

42

Photographer	Arnold Hubbard (UK)
Subject/Location	Rydal Water, Lake District, Cumbria
Camera	Mamyaflex 330
Lens	65mm Sekkor
Film	Ilford FP4

43

Photographer	Martin Deutsch (USA)
Subject/Location	Providence Town Harbour, Mass., USA
Camera	Olympus OM1N
Lens	24mm Zuiko
Film	Kodak Plus-X

44

Photographer	Martin Pope (UK)
Subject/Location	Mime Artist, Adam Darino
Camera	Canon F1
Lens	35mm
Film	Kodak TR1-X

45

Photographer	Jan Sobotka (Czechoslovakia)
Camera	Minolta STR
Lens	30mm
Film	Orwo 400

46

Photographer	Bretislav Marek (Czechoslovakia)

47

Photographer	Bretislav Marek (Czechoslovakia)

48

Photographer	Istudn Gal (Hungary)

49

Photographer	Kari Siren (Finland)

50

Photographer	Jim Hartje (UK)

51

Photographer	Wing Keung Lau (USA)

52

Photographer	Dhiman Bose (India)

53

Photographer	Carolyn Bates (UK)
Camera	Pentax SFX
Lens	28-135mm Zoom
Film	Fujichrome 50

54/55

Photographer	Sylvia Lowe (UK)
Camera	Minolta 7000
Lens	35-70mm Zoom
Film	Kodachrome 25

56/57

Photographer	Ulli Seer/Bob Thomas (Germany/UK)
Camera	Nikonos
Film	Kodachrome 64

58

Photographer	E.A. Janes (UK)
Subject/Location	Gerinuk taken in Sambura National Park, Kenya
Camera	Canon T90
Lens	500mm
Film	Kodachrome 64

59

Photographer	Francisco Marquez (Spain)

60/61

Photographer	Martin Langer (Germany)

62/63

Photographer	Bretislav Marek (Czechoslovakia)

64

Photographer	H.S. Fry (UK)
Subject/Location	Car Boot Sale, Ripley, Surrey
Camera	Nikon F3
Lens	35-105mm Zoom

65

Photographer	Luis Mikowski (Argentina)
Subject/Location	Buenos Aires
Camera	Canon T90
Lens	28mm
Film	Kodak T. Max 400

66/67

Photographer	Janos Eifert (Hungary)
Camera	Pentacon Six
Lens	50mm Flektagon
Film	Orwo NP 27

68/69

Photographer	Gunter Pfutzenreuter (Germany)
Subject/Location	Kurdistan
Camera	Edixa
Lens	135mm
Film	Ilford

70/71

Photographer	Tony Worobiec (UK)
Subject/Location	Favarolles, France
Camera	Mamiya 645s
Lens	35mm
Film	Ilford FP4

72

Photographer	Ron Spillman (UK)
Subject/Location	Michael Leach with Rocky
Camera	Canon EOS 1
Lens	70-210mm Canon Zoom
Film	Ilford 400 Delta

73

Photographer	Ron Spillman (UK)
Subject/Location	Vic Kettle
Camera	Leica R5
Lens	50mm
Film	Agfapan 100

74/75

Photographer	James Soullier (South Africa)
Subject/Location	South Africa
Camera	Leicaflex
Lens	50mm
Film	Kodak T. Max

76

Photographer	Susan Brown (UK)
Subject/Location	Brighton Seafront
Camera	Canon T90
Lens	20mm
Film	Ilford FP4

77

Photographer	Susan Brown (UK)
Subject/Location	Brighton
Camera	Canon T90
Lens	16mm
Film	Ilford FP4

78/79

Photographer	Vaclav Lahovsky (Czechoslovakia)
Camera	Fujica ST 701
Lens	200mm Yashinon
Film	Orwo NP22

80

Photographer	Jagdeep Rajput (India)
Subject/Location	Delhi, India
Camera	Pentax ME Super
Lens	28-80mm Zoom
Film	Orwo NP 27

81

Photographer	David Jones (USA)
Subject/Location	Drying Persian Rugs, Tehran, Iran
Camera	Nikon FTN
Film	Kodachrome 25

82

Photographer	Kenneth Beken (UK)
Subject/Location	'Spirit of J & B' A Class II offshore racing powerboat undergoing trials in a force 8 gale off the Isle of Wight, taken from a Jetranger Helicopter.
Camera	Hasselblad 500 CM
Lens	80mm
Film	Ektachrome 100

83

Photographer	Kenneth Beken (UK)
Subject/Location	'The Card' A Whitbread round the world maxi yacht at the start of the race in the Solent, taken from the 'Beken' 22ft launch.
Camera	Hasselblad 500 CM
Lens	80mm
Film	Ektachrome 100

84

Photographer	Lui Siu Chun (Hong Kong)
Subject/Location	Jura, France
Camera	Canon
Lens	70-210mm Zoom
Film	Fujichrome 100

85

Photographer	Lui Siu Chun (Hong Kong)
Subject/Location	Paris, France
Camera	Canon
Lens	70-210mm Zoom
Film	Fujichrome 100

86

Photographer	Bob Moore (UK)
Subject/Location	Packington Park, Central Warwickshire
Camera	Nikon
Lens	80-200mm
Film	Jessop Slide Film

87

Photographer	J. Winkley (UK)

88/89

Photographer	Victor Glaiman (Argentina)
Subject/Location	Les Halles, Paris
Camera	Canon T90
Film	Agfa XRG 100

90

Photographer	Heather Angel (UK)
Subject/Location	Mother & Cub, Cape Churchill, Canada
Camera	Nikon F4 with thermal jacket
Film	Kodachrome 200

91

Photographer	Heather Angel (UK)
Subject/Location	Cape Churchill, Canada
Camera	Nikon F4 with thermal jacket
Film	Kodachrome 200

92/93

Photographer	Zheng Yun-Feng (China)

94/95

Photographer	John Pyatt
Camera	Pentax MX
Lens	28mm
Film	Fujichrome 100

96

Photographer	Bretislav Marek (Czechoslovakia)

97

Photographer	Michael Lee (UK)
Subject/Location	Harness Raceway, York
Camera	Nikon F3
Lens	80-200mm Nikkor Zoom
Film	Kodak T. Max 200

98/99

Photographer	Don Aston (UK)
Camera	Hasselblad
Lens	80mm Planar
Film	Agfa 100

100

Photographer	Mike Turner (UK)
Camera	Yashica FX-D
Lens	28mm Yashica
Film	Ilford XP5

101

Photographer	Janos Eifert (Hungary)
Camera	Bronica 6 × 6
Lens	150mm
Film	Orwo NP 27

102/103

Photographer	Antonin Streit (Czechoslovakia)

104/105

Photographer	Jim Walker (UK)
Subject/Location	Bavaria, Germany
Camera	Mamiyaflex C330
Lens	80mm
Film	Ilford HP4

106/107

Photographer	Jan Sobotka (Czechoslovakia)
Camera	Minolta STR 101
Lens	200mm
Film	Orwo 400

108

Photographer	Karl Weimar (Germany)
Subject/Location	Wheel Chair Basket Ball Championships
Camera	Canon A1
Lens	80-200mm Tokina Zoom
Film	Kodak T. Max

109

Photographer	Karl Weimer (Germany)
Subject/Location	Wheel Chair Marathon
Camera	Canon A1
Lens	80-200mm Tokina Zoom
Film	Ilford XP1

110

Photographer	Mark Hakanson (UK)
Subject/Location	Friern Barnet Town Fair, England
Camera	Canon
Lens	20mm
Film	Kodak T. Max

111

Photographer	John Eubank (Canada)
Camera	Pentax MX
Lens	35mm
Film	Kodak TRI.X

112

Photographer	Luis Mikowski (Argentina)
Subject/Location	Buenos Aires
Camera	Canon A1
Lens	50mm
Film	Kodak TRI.X

113

Photographer	John Pyatt (UK)
Camera	Pentax MX
Lens	28mm
Film	Fujichrome 100

114/115

Photographer	Szamody Zsolt (Hungary)

116

Photographer **Mike Hollist (UK)**
Camera **Nikon F3**
Lens **85mm**
Film **Kodak Gold 1600**

117

Photographer **John Candelario (USA)**
Subject/Location **'Lep-Jag' – Las Vegas**
Camera **Canon**
Lens **28-70mm Canon Zoom**
Film **Kodak Gold 200**

118

Photographer **Keith Vaughan (Canada)**

119

Photographer **Ines Roberts (USA)**
Subject/Location **River formation in Slot Canyon, Arizona, USA**
Camera **Minolta XD5**
Lens **70-210mm Zoom**
Film **Fujichrome 50**

120/121

Photographer **Ricardo Torossian (Argentina)**
Subject/Location **Lake Titacaca**
Camera **Minolta XG9**
Film **Fujichrome 100**

122

Photographer **Leo Mason (UK)**
Camera **Nikon**
Lens **18mm**
Film **Fujichrome 50 Velvia**

123

Photographer **Bretislav Marek (Czechoslovakia)**

124

Photographer **Zheng Yun-Feng (China)**

125

Photographer **L.S. Tak (India)**

126

Photographer **Brian Watt (UK)**

127

Photographer **Bill Ivy (Canada)**
Subject/Location **Eyes of a Horsefly**
Camera **Canon F1**
Film **Kodachrome 64**

128

Photographer **Rajendar Joshi (India)**
Subject/Location **Matheran, India**
Camera **Minolta SRl-101**
Lens **28-135mm Zoom**
Film **Kodachrome 100**

129

Photographer **Rajan Kapoor (India)**
Subject/Location **New Delhi**
Camera **Minolta 8000i**
Lens **100-300mm Zoom**
Film **Kodak T. Max 400**

130

Photographer **Janusz Filipczak (Poland)**
Camera **Minolta X300**
Lens **35-70mm Zoom**
Film **Orwo NP20**

131

Photographer **Don MacLellan (UK)**
Camera **Rolleiflex SLX**
Lens **150mm**
Film **Ilford 100**

132

Photographer **Rudolf Hillebrand (Germany)**
Camera **Nikon F2**
Lens **55mm**
Film **Kodak Infrared**

133

Photographer **Rudolf Hillebrand (Germany)**
Camera **Nikon F2**
Lens **85mm**
Film **Kodak Infrared**

134

Photographer **Rudy Lewis (UK)**
Subject/Location **Las Paz (Bolivia)**
Camera **Nikon F2**
Lens **85mm**
Film **Kodak TR1 X**

135

Photographer **Rudy Lewis (UK)**
Subject/Location **Peru**
Camera **Nikon F2**
Lens **85mm**
Film **Kodak TR1 X**

136/137

Photographer **Peter Gennard (UK)**
Subject/Location **Stourbridge, West Midlands**
Camera **Nikon FE**
Lens **35-105mm Nikkor Zoom**
Film **Ilford HP5**

138/139

Photographer **Frantsek Dostal (Czechoslovakia)**
Camera **Minolta SRT 303**
Lens **35mm Rokkor**
Film **Orwo NP22**

140

Photographer **Ted Simkins (UK)**
Subject/Location **York Minster**
Camera **Ricoh KR10**
Lens **135mm Tamron**
Film **Ilford FP4**

141

Photographer **Damian Davies (UK)**
Camera **Minolta X700**
Lens **85mm Vivitar**
Film **Ilford HP5**

142

Photographer **Joan Wakelin (UK)**
Subject/Location **Bristol**
Camera **Canon AE1**
Lens **24mm**
Film **Ilford HP5**

143

Photographer **Mike Turner (UK)**
Subject/Location **Dame Alicia Markova at the Ilkley Ballet School**
Camera **Contax**
Lens **50mm Zeiss**
Film **Kodak T.Max 400**

144

Photographer **Bill Finn (UK)**
Subject/Location **European Sidecar Championship at Bridgenorth**
Camera **Canon T90**
Lens **70-110mm Canon Zoom**

145

Photographer **Keith Vaughan (Canada)**

146

Photographer **Bill Ivy (Canada)**
Subject/Location **Young Red Squirrels**
Camera **Canon F1**
Lens **100mm**
Film **Kodachrome 64**

147

Photographer **Bill Ivy (Canada)**
Subject/Location **Mother Racoon with Kids**
Camera **Canon F1**
Lens **300mm**
Film **Kodachrome 64**

148/149

Photographer — Janos Stekovics (Yugoslavia)
Subject/Location — Romania

150

Photographer — Akira Aoki (Japan)
Subject/Location — Shirane Volcano, Nagano, Japan
Camera — Hasselblad 500 C/M
Lens — 350mm Tele-Tessar

151 (Upper)

Photographer — Akira Aoki (Japan)
Subject/Location — Takayama, Gifu, Japan
Camera — Canon EOS 1
Lens — 300mm Canon

151 (Lower)

Photographer — Akira Aoki (Japan)
Subject/Location — Murasaki-No, Kyoto, Japan
Camera — Canon EOS 1
Lens — 300mm Canon

152/153

Photographer — David Johnston (UK)
Subject/Location — Telford, West Midlands
Camera — Canon F1
Lens — 24mm
Film — Kodachrome 64

154

Photographer — Jack Jackson (UK)
Subject/Location — Wreck of the 'Umbria' in Red Sea

155 (Upper)

Photographer — Jack Jackson (UK)
Subject/Location — Grey Reef Shark, Red Sea

155 (Lower)

Photographer — Jack Jackson (UK)
Subject/Location — Tigerfish, Red Sea

156/157

Photographer — George Morris (UK)
Subject/Location — Grindelwald, Switzerland
Camera — Nikon FM
Lens — 200mm Nikkor
Film — Ektacolor 160

158

Photographer — Shivji (India)
Subject/Location — Jodhpur, India

159

Photographer — Eric Bird (UK)
Subject/Location — Morocco

160

Photographer — Ricky Teoh (Malaysia)
Camera — Nikon
Lens — 200mm
Film — Konica

161

Photographer — Bob Moore (UK)

162

Photographer — Jim Walker (UK)
Subject/Location — Toulouse, France
Camera — Mamiyaflex C330
Lens — 180mm
Film — Ilford FP4

163

Photographer — A.G. Hill (UK)
Subject/Location — Bourbonne Les Bains (France)
Camera — Zeiss Ikonta
Film — Ilford FP4

164

Photographer — Vaclav Lahovsky (Czechoslovakia)
Camera — Fujica ST 701
Lens — 35mm
Film — Orwo NP22

165

Photographer — Vaclkav Lahovsky (Czechoslovakia)
Camera — Fujica ST 701
Lens — 200mm
Film — Orwo NP20

166

Photographer — David Tully (UK)
Camera — Canon T90
Lens — 500mm
Film — Kodak T.Max 400

167

Photographer — Martin Pope (UK)
Camera — Canon F1
Lens — 200mm
Film — Kodak TR1 X

168/169

Photographer — Peter Hallam (UK)
Subject/Location — Malahide, Dublin
Camera — Olympus OM1 N
Lens — 24mm
Film — Ilford HP5

170/171

Photographer — Ricardo Torossian (Argentina)
Subject/Location — Peru
Camera — Minolta XG
Film — Kodak TR1 X

172/173

Photographer — Zseni Jung (Hungary)
Camera — Mamiya RB 67
Lens — 90mm
Film — Orwo NP20

174/175

Photographer — Gennadi Karchewski (USSR)
Camera — Zenit
Lens — 50mm

176

Photographer — Gontran Chamard (Canada)
Subject/Location — Westmount Park, Montreal
Camera — Nikon FE
Lens — 24mm
Film — Ilford XP1

177

Photographer — Bob Green (UK)
Camera — Bronica ETR
Lens — 40mm
Film — Fujichrome 100

178

Photographer — Roger Reynolds (UK)
Subject/Location — Puffin with Sand Eels

179 (Upper)

Photographer — Kian Choong Lee (Singapore)
Camera — Nikon F2
Lens — 75-105mm Zoom
Film — Ektachrome 64

179 (Lower)

Photographer — John Bingley (UK)

180

Photographer — Anthony Blake (UK)
Subject/Location — Tokyo Fishmarket
Camera — Leica M6
Lens — 75mm
Film — Kodachrome 200

181

Photographer — Anthony Blake (UK)
Subject/Location — Tokyo Fishmarket
Camera — Leica M6
Lens — 35mm
Film — Kodachrome 200

	182
Photographer	Peter Siviter (UK)
Subject/Location	Cyprus
Camera	Canon EOS 600
Lens	24mm
Film	Kodachrome 64

	183
Photographer	Peter Gedeon (Hungary)
Lens	Nikkor 16mm
Film	Fujichrome

	184/185
Photographer	Roger Reynolds (UK)
Subject/Location	Camel Market, Pushkar, India

	186
Photographer	Van Greaves (UK)
Subject/Location	Birmingham, England
Camera	Nikon F801
Lens	70-300mm Vivitar Zoom

	187 (Upper)
Photographer	Van Greaves (UK)
Subject/Location	Birmingham, England
Camera	Nikon F801
Lens	28-105mm Zoom

	187 (Lower)
Photographer	David Johnston (UK)
Subject/Location	Birmingham, England
Camera	Canon F1
Lens	17mm Canon
Film	Kodachrome 64

	188
Photographer	Paul Ridsdale (UK)
Subject/Location	The camera was clamped to the bonnet and remote control cable fired
Camera	Nikon FM2
Lens	17mm
Film	Fujichrome 100

	189
Photographer	Mike Stacey (UK)

	190/191
Photographer	Colin Westage (UK)

	192
Photographer	J.W. Dettmer (Germany)

	193
Photographer	Fredrik Persson (Sweden)
Subject/Location	Belleville, Paris
Camera	Leica M3
Lens	50mm
Film	Kodak TR1 X

	194/195
Photographer	Tony Butcher (UK)
Subject/Location	Canon T90
Camera	90mm Tamron
Lens	Ilford FP 4

	196/197
Photographer	Vasily Titov (USSR)

	198/199
Photographer	Howard Walker (UK)
Subject/Location	Hong Kong
Camera	Nikon F3
Lens	80-200mm Zoom
Film	Ilford HP5

	200/201
Photographer	Ivan Cisar (Czechoslovakia)

	202
Photographer	Mark Smith (UK)
Subject/Location	B.B. King in Norwich
Camera	Canon F1
Lens	50mm
Film	Kodak TR1 X

	203
Photographer	Joan Wakelin (UK)
Camera	Canon AE1
Lens	24mm
Film	Ilford XP1

	204/205
Photographer	Mike Mathias (Canada)
Subject/Location	Stoufville, Ontario
Camera	Canon F1
Lens	70-210 Zoom
Film	Ilford FP4

	206
Photographer	H.F. Keeling (UK)
Subject/Location	Wolverhampton Shopping Centre
Camera	Canon A1
Lens	200mm Vivitar
Film	Kodak T.Max 400

	207
Photographer	H.F. Keeling (UK)
Subject/Location	Wolverhampton
Camera	Canon A1
Lens	100mm
Film	Kodak T.Max 400

	208
Photographer	Owen Evans (UK)
Subject/Location	Wales
Camera	Pentax MX
Lens	18mm
Film	Ilford FP4

	209
Photographer	Laurie Campbell (UK)
Subject/Location	Rannock Moor
Camera	Nikon F3
Lens	28mm
Film	Kodachrome 64

	210
Photographer	Rudolf Herbst (Hungary)

	211
Photographer	C.D. Patel (UK)
Camera	Nikon FA
Lens	70-210mm Zoom
Film	Ektachrome 50

	212
Photographer	Stephen Chape (UK)
Subject/Location	Whitburn, Scotland
Camera	Nikon F3
Lens	24mm
Film	Kodachrome 64

	213
Photographer	G.R.S. Grimshaw (UK)
Subject/Location	Lake Windermere
Camera	Olympus OM10
Lens	50mm
Film	Kodachrome 54

	214/215
Photographer	Claudio Marcozzi (San Marino)

	216/217
Photographer	P. Glyn-Jones (UK)
Subject/Location	Fish Tail Mountain, Machapucare, Nepal
Camera	Nikon F301
Lens	28-200mm Zoom

	218
Photographer	Bob Martin (Allsport) (UK)
Subject/Location	Balloon Over Bristol
Camera	Nikon

219

Photographer   **Bob Mossel (Australia)**

220

Photographer   **John Grey (UK)**

221

Photographer   **Tony Barnes (UK)**
Subject/Location   **Bognor Regis**
Camera   **Pentax SFX**
Lens   **35-70mm Zoom**
Film   **Fujichrome**

222/223

Photographer   **M.R. Owaisi (Pakistan)**

224

Photographer   **Miklos Juhasz (Hungary)**

Backend Paper

Photographer   **Arnold Hubbard (UK)**
Subject/Location   **Swaledale, Yorkshire**
Camera   **Mamiyaflex 330**
Lens   **65mm**
Film   **Ilford FP4**